Rat and Cat

in

Let's Jump!

Written by
Jeanne Willis

Illustrated by
Gabriele Antonini

Rat was looking at the TV.

"Got you!" said Cat.

"Let me go and we can
jump on the bed!" said Rat.

"OK," said Cat.
He let Rat go.

"I can get up here," said Rat.

"I can do flips! Can you
do flips Cat?" said Rat.

"If you can, I can," said Cat.
He went up too.

"Go on Cat. Jump off," said Rat.

"Look at this flip," said Cat.

Down, down, down went Cat!
Up, up, up went Rat ...
up into a tree!

"That flip was a flop!" said Rat.
"I will get you Rat!" said Cat.